SHARING WATER BY THE RIVER

POEMS OF THE FEAST

DENHAM GRIERSON

COVENTRY
PRESS

Published in Australia by
Coventry Press
33 Scoresby Road
Bayswater Vic. 3153
Australia

ISBN 9780648566137

Copyright © Denham Grierson 2019

Cataloguing-in-Publication entry is available from the National Library of Australia
http://catalogue.nla.gov.au/.

Cover design by Ian James - www.jgd.com.au
Text design by Filmshot Graphics (FSG)

Printed in Australia

CONTENTS

FOREWORD

Poems of the Feast – and what a feast! I just could not put them down, until I had read and absorbed them all! No domestic chores that afternoon!

I remember Rev. Bruce Prewer, poet and liturgist, being told of his prayers that they weren't religious enough, and before they were published he had to add more "God" language. I guess if you have a Rev. in front of your name, publishers expect you to write about God. Well, in this collection you won't find too many words about "God", but you will find poems that speak about things of the Spirit and human spirituality.

Denham Grierson often told me that we need to live with ambiguity and paradox in life and in faith – even in our understanding of God. These poems are full of awareness of both ambiguity and paradox, and many carry for me a "sting in the tail" that surprises and challenges, emotionally and intellectually.

> Here there is a binding
> Knitting together a decisiveness
> Threads of ambiguity
> Secured into a deciding centre
> Where slowly there grows
> A sense of identifiable inter-action

(Tapestry)

The grouping of the poems into "before, during, after" takes us on a spiritual journey and into deeper and deeper meanings. The "after" poems offer surprising resources for worship planners as they craft worship experiences around the annual liturgical celebrations.

The reader will find here much to stimulate and to enable reflection. There is no chance of being bored with this collection. They grow out of Denham's life experiences that often echo our own, and the wisdom he shares from a lifetime of reflecting-on-experience (after Paulo Freire). To mis-quote a well-known saying, a life lived without reflecting-on-experience is a life not lived, because there will be no learning, just repetition year after year. There is much learning embedded in these exquisitely crafted poems, and much to learn from their wisdom.

Denham's rich life experiences are clearly the source of his poetic imagery. He finds food for thought in reflecting on such things as a ceiling fan, retirement, walking stick, McDonalds, kindred, war zones, Queens College, Digger, to name a few.

> No one forgets how to ride a bicycle
> Gripping the handlebars comes easily
> Slipping onto the seat
> Feet unerringly finding the pedals
> The first gut wrenching effort
> To get inert wheels moving...
>
> Now with the wind in my face
> Sparkles flying from glinting spokes
> Pursued by remembered shouts
> Of teenage enthusiasm
> At eighty-one, caution thrown to the wind
> I hurtle downhill once again with uncertain brakes.

(Bicycle)

There is balance in these poems between seriousness and fun, sadness and joy, and all points along these continua, again reflecting the personality of the poet. (For example *Dr Boreham's*

Pyjamas, Emu, Mirror Image.) I also found here poems to feed my concerns for justice (*for example Waiting, Wall*), for reconciliation in this land (*Kindred, Thief, Lava Tubes, 60,00 Years Old*) and for meeting the current political challenges (*Gap, Shadowland, Profit for All, Otherwise, Pollution*).

For those who are yearning for new and different understandings of God, and expressions of their faith, spirits will be lifted in these pages, like a cup overflowing with wisdom and encouragement.

> Gossamer drift of spider threads
> Across a summer sky
> A binding that wraps the blue heavens
> Into a gift to hold
>
> There is hidden in the spectral drift
> A crafted message spun
> The inner being of God's web
> Sensitive to the slightest touch…
>
> The smallest impulse
> Reaching to touch the infinite

(Spider Moment)

For others who don't claim a particular faith label or ways of expressing the meanings of their life journey, spirituality will be nurtured in joyful echoes and deep whispers of their own stirrings.

> Against the liminal edge, a deep red terminus, rectangle
> Fringes at north-south ends, reaching further out

I walk, sinking into an oriental mind
Mystical, complex, holding all things in balance
By some elusive beauty of spirit flowing
Endlessly beneath my feet

(Silk carpet)

And so I look at my Persian carpet... and remember the Moorish designs of the Alhambra, the other buildings in Spanish cities visited with a beloved son, the awe of being in the largest mosque in the world and the horror of its "desecration" by an ornate Christian church within. The history of centuries of three faiths living together sharing culture, food, architecture, and the rejection that followed, all bound up in a carpet! Wow, Denham! A new appreciation of what I walk on every day, awakened by these words.

So, thank you, Denham, for penning these words and for giving me the privilege of writing the Foreword. In the poems I have found threads of your life and mine intertwining, and the warmth of our relationship that has contributed to the warp and weft of the rich tapestry of my journey - from planned to unplanned, known to unknown and back again, from certainty to surprise, ignorance to knowledge, experience to the beginning of wisdom. Thank you for sharing your wisdom with me along the way with its ups and downs, ins and outs, lines and circles.

There are more to come, I know, because your brain never stops its creativity! I look forward to the next collection!

Marell Hansin

INTRODUCTION

Poets know that they do not write poetry. They write poetry down. A poem frequently comes fully formed. All that needs to be done is record it with only superficial amendment. The complex sources of this epiphany are both conscious and unconscious, bringing into being clarifying moments of existence. It is difficult to argue with that which has its own integrity, its own profundity, its own purpose. When a poem comes to rest, it breaks open new understandings if we choose to participate in its offering. It brings a gift. Much like welcoming a stranger in who speaks a new language that unlocks the mystery of your own deepest convictions.

In the process, what is revealed is the symbiotic relationship between the old and the new, freeing us from that powerless state where we know more than we can tell, for we do not have the words. Here is the gift of poetry, the transmission of existence clarification.

There is communion in this faerie process, illuminated by the image of sharing water by the river. Imagine after a long walking journey that you pause in a camping ground by a river. After washing hands and face in a moment of refreshment, you are approached by campers, husband and wife, with a long cold glass of water. They invite you to share a meal with them.

Barbecued sausages arrive wrapped in bread, spread with tomato sauce and onion rings. Here, in this cameo moment, the celebration of shared experience. 'You are on a journey', the host says, looking at your discarded backpack. You nod. 'As we all are'. 'What have you learned?' Conversation begins. Telling stories by the vast flowing river that sustains us is what we do. At that feast, poetry brings provision that opens up the meaning of what we seek to know, and, by its agency, are able to tell. There is an enfolding hospitality in the telling that brings life. As surely as the water drawn from the flowing source of all created things, poetry is a bearer of the gift of life.

ACKNOWLEDGMENTS

Thanks are due to a group of people who are not only competent professionals but also valued friends. To Marelle Harisun, learned colleague and longtime friend, for her generous and affirming foreword.

Hugh McGinlay, who is the most trusted of editors and valued colleague.

My wife, Mavis, who again undertook copy editing, as readily and as competently as ever, and my daughter, Su, who took the photograph for the back cover with her usual serendipity.

My grateful thanks also to Coventry Press who are willing not only to give support to authors but to publish them as well.

No boat is safely launched unless it has a competent and committed crew. We sail joyously together.

BEFORE

LILIES

The deep pink lilies
Open with winter heating
Perfume permeates our living room
As if a presence has settled there

Dusky pink beauty upon
Crisply folded leaves
Deep green sustaining
Image of tableau perfection

So we are addressed
In the twilight fade
Of the winter day
Beauty has its own conversation

ESSENCE

There is little to be said in the end
Since that which matters
Transcends knowledge

It is difficult to accept
That not knowing
Is the true gift

How hard to learn
That all we secure
Will mist-like drift away

What will remain
Cannot be banked
For love is priceless

We are left without understanding
As an act of mercy
That we might understand

DR BOREHAM'S PYJAMAS

The famed Baptist preacher Dr Boreham
Always acted with saintly decorum
Unlike tigers, lions and lamas
He slept after lunch in pyjamas

Overcoming a preacher's end game
He conquered his hereditary name
Speaking boldly, sending people bananas
He slept after lunch in pyjamas

He rose to exegetical fame
Despite the curse of his name
Without using papas or mamas
He slept after lunch in pyjamas

I have only respect for his actions
Despite the anti and pro factions
I would like to follow this panorama
But somebody lost his pyjamas

WAITING

Again in a queue waiting
Counting those who are ahead
Looking for a sense of meaning
Wondering what is going to be said

All of us summoned by the system
Remorseless the civic rule
Following the laid out pattern
Searching for a sinning soul

CentreLink prepares its edict
Anxious faces, grim
Gathered to hear a judgment
Celebrative outcome slim

We wait in a cocoon of silence
Walled within an anxious square
Subject to unthinking menace
Waiting for reality's harsh fare

Fearful of a social breach
Devoid of reassuring speech
I sit upon the judgment bench
Freedom's gift beyond my reach

EMU

You may cast around
With your beady eye
From the exalted nest
Of the coat of arms
Imperiously looking over Australia
With a measure of indifference

You have been walking country
For centuries untold
Spindly legs, knobby knees
Kicking up red dust
At high speed
To little real effect

You were honoured
Given a task to do
Not to gather in surly mobs
But to create a future
To offer vision
To call into being a new world

So step up
It is high time
You learnt to fly

CEILING FAN

Our ceiling fan spins
Black and white flashes
Symbiotically united

The only options
Lesser or greater speed
Without respite

Casting upon the ceiling
A dark stain of shadow
Declaring our life's struggle

Spinning with mesmerising effect
Moving air across the room
For no permanent result

Set in place
Are inescapable dynamics
Of endless circling

Unless, of course, one turns
To contemplate the still axis
Around which life moves

RETIREMENT

The electric butlers of our digital age
Enhance the non-practical matter of just being
Mediating life as entertainment or tourism
Bowling green levelling pleasure-pain polarities
By attention to short term self interest

They do not understand there is no cure for life
Organically constructed, the cards dealt eons ago
We live the inescapable. A life not felt would need no cure
A life felt but unexamined would have no meaning
So here we are, caught in reflection's web they call retirement

WALKING STICK

Smooth, polished shaft, rubber tipped
Grip shaped to be grasped
Strong companion of uncertain feet
Assurance in steadiness held fast

Not just an aid or comfort tool
Sun-dial, a measurement of time
Completing the riddle of the Sphinx
Four legs, two legs, three legs assigned

To be trustingly leant on, rested by the side
Friend in a space of flexibility denied

NEWNESS

They do not want my poems
Not biblical enough they say
Fearing lostness if they roam
The child inside who cannot play

Knock on wood, someone should
Try a rhyme all the same
Do not fear the random word
Learn again to play a game

Look for threads among the old
Seek direction in the new
Skipping down the trodden path
Old shoes wet with morning dew

THE SMALL HOURS

But there is forgiveness with you, so that you may be revered

Psalm 130:4

In the small hours the Hobyahs come creeping
Insubstantial shades of actions passed
Calling up memories of missed soul meetings
Choices mishandled, relationships that failed
Disturbing the small hours

Sleep, not to be snared, slides silently away
The visitation calls forth long-held regrets
None redeemable, all of them still present
Rising from a sub-conscious vault
Released in the small hours

They enter into dialogue, for what purpose
Nothing can be changed, no matter deep remorse
Laid bare in inquisition our condition
Not able to expunge the bad or worse
Numbered in the small hours

The memories sting, despite regret
Listing love's failure, love's expression
Un-given in relationship to loved ones
Those life itself, unacknowledged
Transparent in the small hours

Spectres speak of relationships
Memory has no power to dismiss
It is so, no going back
The voices worry, fret and whisper
Unanswerable in the small hours

Saved only by the word
That speaks forgiveness
Received with thankfulness
Forgiveness's undeserved gift
Redeeming the small hours

THE PAST

The past is a far country
Signs read 'No Entry'

Far crows cawing, dryness and dust
Old farm machinery covered in rust

Landscape in which dreams were lost
Not spring's enchantment but winter's frost

Events fixed in time's amber
Dried arrangements eliciting wonder

Paintings completed, varnished to set
No movement detected, the hour glass spent

Photos, sketches, faces and traces
Memory struggles to recall times and places

Jigsaw pieces of precious things
Vanity box, lockets, medallions and rings

Concealing pretence, deceit, and lies
Record completed as time's arrow flies

Tapestry, splendid, impressive, profound
In now's bright light ground of my ground

MCDONALDS

We sit in a back room
Consuming cups of early morning theology
Capitalism's well-oiled engine purring
With skilful ingenuity around us
Guiding streams of breakfast hunger
To waiting stations of consumption
Ears budded to unfocused music
Calling awareness into consciousness
Craving energy from coffee cups and
Warm, salt-sprinkled bags

In the back room we know a deeper hunger
Unpicking threads of morning wonder
Woven into the rhythm of existence
That anything exists at all
The mystery beyond telling
Sharing thought's bread
Drinking reflection's wine
Undisciplined by commercial zeal
Seeking also to gather energy
Celebrating a different feast of days

KINDRED

There is a sense of wanting
A current pushing on
A windless pause enlarging
What then to gaze upon

There is a distance hazing
Without clarifying speech
What is the glance concealing
How touch its hiddenness

There is a yawning gap
Uncrossed by any treaty
Too far for any running jump
Where lies a bridge of unity

There is a vacuum rife
That does not transmit meaning
Without oxygen to give us life
How then to share our dreaming

The beating heart, the flowing blood
The urgent hope, the sharpened eye
Kindred in this sunburnt land
Silent beneath a cloudless sky

MYSTERY

Mystery in its word-origin
Closed eyes, closed mouth
Its hiddenness beyond sight
Evading the efficacy of words
Immutable in its singularity
Communicating nonetheless
Remaining undiminished
Even in the giving

Tangible yet
As indivisible as smoke
Hard to conceive with open eyes
Articulate with open mouth
We talk about our selves
That which is eternally elusive
The enigma of being

THIEF

That which is concealed
Will be revealed of course
Secrecy cannot be maintained
In a conscious multiverse

We cannot run away
Responsibility is to another
Honour our common way
Caring for Earth mother

Fire regenerates the land
Burning ash the precious lie
If we would see renewal
Racist philosophy must die

We cannot avoid awareness
We possess what is not ours
Making a sacred law of progress
Our right to own disputed land

Make our nation great by all means
Outcome of the deal and gun
Do not wonder in the judgment
Why all purpose is undone

Dispossession is the answer
To the trauma of the soul
Music of the spirit-dancer
Give up what your nation stole

TAPESTRY

In the drifting between
Convergence and divergence
Affirmation and rejection
Identity and disassociation
There is an intuitive space
Of raw becoming

Here there is a binding
Knitting together a decisiveness
Threads of ambiguity
Secured into a deciding centre
Where slowly there grows
A sense of identifiable inter-action

This island of being makes possible
A sense of self that grows
Inter-twined with the stranger's otherness
Compound of light and shadow
Truth and falsehood, success and failure
Giving to the tapestry its unique beauty

NEWS

The news is good
Red riding hood
The news is nice
Three blind mice
The news has shocks
Goldilocks
The news is slow
Pinocchio
The news is simply that
Jack Spratt
The news is nasty still
Jack and Jill
The news is building walls
Humpty Dumpty will surely fall
The news not understood
Which the trees, which the wood
News about the times
Just nursery rhymes

TRAIN

Powered by lithium batteries $30,000 each
The tourist train moves with slow deliberation
Along the two kilometre Busselton pier
The longest wooden pier in the world

The commentary is enlightening
'You could not have this experience
 Anywhere else in the world'
So totally undeniable
Its philosophical force irresistible

Out to the end, nine metres deep
Return to the shallows of ordinary experience
Overwhelmed by knowing
I could not do this anywhere else in the world

GAP

There is a slipping away of trust
A lack of belief in civic foundations
Confidence declining in the body politic
Disappearing civility in social commerce

The giant octopus of economics
Expelling black ink into our lives
Concealing what truly takes place
In the swirling currents of our hopefulness

Beneath the cloudless sun drenched sky
Large ancient boulders rest
Down from towering volcanic peaks
Frozen by time's forgetfulness
As wild flower colours flourish
In organic splendour across the moor

Indifferent to our human dilemma
Of how to match the unrestrained power
Of the sea with a potter's shaping
To turn the uncontrolled intensity
Into a vessel in which the wine
That brings succour can be poured
In sacramental promise

Restoring what is lost
Making the broken moment whole
Building the city with justice
Releasing actions of renewal and beauty

Bringing to the holy place
Gifts to honour a renewing God
Whose spirit runs as free
As this bounding, breaking wave fest
Beneath my feet

ABSENCE

The God who left us
Was the clay fashioning
Of creative hunger
Into which pins could be thrust
To fulfil a meaning lust

The God who vanished
Into glacial endlessness
Of cold space
Had no form in any case
To fit within our time and place

The ravening Deity
Who stripped the flesh
From wilful bones
Judging us for wantonness
Perished for lack of humanness

Above story, chapter, verse
King of the Universe
Died alone
Subjects turned away
Disavowing royal display

Deus Abscondis never lost
Never found, Being's host
Words strain
To define ineffable
Beyond the measurable

Absent Other always present
Invisible icon, ether veined
Vacuum empty, presence filled
Grandeur of the active passive
Absence's touch the true possessive

ESCAPE

The dread of evil
Has few antidotes
None of them effective
In the moment of address

Hunger for the poor man
Has no release
Nemesis is not the name
Of freedom's peace

But in the things that bloom
The seeds of life that grow
In secret, heart-breaking joy
God's promise flows

TWILIGHT

In evening's dusk I sit on a village seat
A distant fountain sending water tumbling
Singing its joyous melody

I felt the earth, old bones creaking
Turning slowly and with effort
To complete another circuit

Above a garland of stars twinkle
Nestling in their velvet cloak
I am, once again, among friends

SURPRISE!

Synoptic problem, which the scholar's name
Oral tradition bears much of the blame
Contrariness, few views the same
Dissembling truth that leads deceitfully to fame

Shaped by the highly polished story
Out of the dust, ascending to the heights of glory
Passing over spilled blood and all things gory
Patting together cupcakes saying sorry

From the graveyard, end of crucifixion
A place of doubt and troubling confusion
An unsuspected life transfusion
Out of the abyss a resurrection

SHADOW

Even in bright sun
There our shadow
Stalks us

Tied to feet and hands
Implicit in every step
Following every gesture

Companion of the way
It makes no demand
But claims its place

As time passes
It becomes larger
Obscuring where we have been

If we are blind to it
Our shadow, weightless,
Weighs us down to victimhood

Others see its following
Influence and effect
When we do not

At high noon crucifixion
It waits, emerging, we learn
Blanketing the earth with darkness

It has no power
I share it with you
Sometimes we need shade

It imitates life only
Out of darkness
Life will come again

WAR ZONE

She lives her life at periscope depth
Alert and wary
Pursuing paths by stealth
Suspecting mines in the complimentary

All her missions quiet and hidden
Fighting unseen currents
Moving as one bidden
Protecting deep held secrets

Living in a war zone
Outcome of a hostile sexual act
Reacting to intelligence alone
Without hope of amnesty or pact

I remember radiant youth
A child of gladness fully alive
Chaos of inner panic, south
Incoming threat, dive, dive, dive

MOVING ON

At the beginning faith comes alive
In the seat of the emotions
An overwhelming feeling dependence
An all-encompassing, accepting troth
Engaging every humming string
In the first stage of love's embrace

Time calls forth, inevitably, a second stage
Seeking for reasons for this cascading hope
Trying to establish a secure ground
That can defend the treasure against
Doubting hordes, always at the gate,
Seeking to overthrow what seems ridiculous

There is, at the closing down end
Of life's journey, a third stage
That recognises emotion and reason
Never can resolve in any final form
Old questions reborn, new questions springing forth
Like armed men from the earth

A nevertheless that stands against the affront
Which declares life's futility, its meaninglessness
No more than autumn leaves swept away by time's river
Into a bare Winter's cold
A Will to believe in the very court of doubt
A choice which says convinced, Here I will stand

In the unresolved still live the early certainties
The wind crack in the spread sails swings the boat

Forward, the rudder guiding through the wave wrack
And sea mist to the harbour briefly glimpsed
Where on the beach a figure stands, fish, damper, wine
Waiting for the feast's commencement, shared joy

So we return to the beginning where it all began
Understanding fully for the first time
We have never been lost but always found
Firmly held when fearing life slip through our fingers
Recognising in the everydayness of this feast
The grasp of love. This is where we have been bound

DURING

GLOVE

The glove covers the hand
Shadows its every movement
Warms it in the cold
Protects it from disfigurement

The glove covers the hand
Skin to its very skin
Patterned to its shape
Enfolding all within

Nearer than hands and feet
Closer than breathing
The spirit discreet
Being of my being

The glove covers the hand
One with its creation
Blueprint carefully planned
To mirror every action

Before, above, beneath, behind
There is the shadow found
No gesture futile in the end
The glove covers the hand

LAVA TUBES

We wrote to our friends
We stand on your ancestral lands
On the morrow
We will enter the lava tubes
At Undara
Whisper your names
Give news to the listeners
Offer our respect

So it was, in the millennium flowing
Of Rainbow Snake creation
We had our conversation
Leaving with deep music
From the rock birthing passage
Stepping out into Australian sun
Smelling the thank you eucalyptus
Of the flowering gums

THE ETERNAL NOW

The option is
It seems
Now or too late
We cannot recover
That which has been
The not yet
Escapes our grasp
The ferry leaves at six
You are either on it
Or not

In a break
I told her how wonderful
Her singing was
'Thank you' she said
Touching my cheek
As I sat down
It came to me
That the song is now
The epiphany followed
Now is forever

THE GHOST WHO WALKS

In the bricolage of the bottom drawer
I found a Phantom ring
Skull and crossbones intact, child size
When life was simple, a mysterious hero
Who left a sign of terror on
The jaw of unconscious villains
A time when, above ambiguity
It was possible to be triumphant
If one was 'a ghost who walked'
Accompanied by jungle drums
All focused in this magic ring
I have never managed to fit my finger

WALL

The wall, symbol of our failure
To recognise shared humanness
Stretches across continents, divides
Back gardens, protects inner space
Shadow fear of the other
Holding it up

On the other side all that threatens
Unknown and menacing
Terrain occupied by our unresolved self
Which leaps the wall to pose
As all that must be resisted, wasteland
Populated by what we cannot face within

That which separates, divides, is diabolic
That which gathers, nurtures, its antidote
On the border industrious demons
Building higher, disease of our isms
Becoming more solid, more divisive
Creating the breeding ground for new enemies

SPIDER MOMENT

Gossamer drift of spider threads
Across a summer sky
A binding that wraps the blue heavens
Into a gift to hold

There is hidden in the spectral drift
A crafted message spun
The inner being of God's web
Sensitive to the slightest touch

The smallest impulse
Reaching to touch the infinite
Registers on this frail tapestry
Enfolding the vast sky

A tremor, as gentle as breath
Is not lost in trackless waste
But held, this spider moment
Forever in God's grasp

SHADOWLAND

There is a shadowland of awareness
Teeming with unfulfilled newness
Pre-conscious its natural terrain
Imaginative fantasies, bubbling metaphors
Birthing the un-restrained
Erupting into focus in the small hours

There is a summons to pay attention
The editing of daily expectation
Freshly made over by anarchy
Of a dissembling kind
Seeking to change the way of thinking
That marches with the band

This is a deep moving hidden current
A pre-natal insistence that preparation
Be made to greet a fresh patterning
Of our way of being human
Elevating what is subsidiary to focal accord
Gentler meaning, outreaching care, all stories heard

SPELL

You would be forgiven for believing
That all things conspired to make
The moment of encounter eternally designed

Such was the magic of the meeting
In which all that mattered
Was said without words

Elusiveness lay in the between
A sense of immensity
Of the one and the other

So totally encompassing
As to place all options
In a row stretching for ever

Shaped, moulded, crafted
Measured, sustained, defined
Held in a moment lasting a lifetime

ASHES

They sang in the darkened streets
As the great Cathedral burned
Bound by a culture that gathered them
Into a proud people, the emblem of
Their unity ruined before their eyes
Their identity stronger in the flames

The Chinese dragon belching fire and smoke
Has fallen upon Uighur holy places
Destroying 700 mosques, hollowing out a culture
Re-designing whole cities for maximum surveillance
Reducing the symbols of a shared identity
Of a whole people to rubble and scorched earth

If religion is the essence of culture
Culture the form of religion then
Here the very soul of a civilisation
Is being systematically destroyed, an act of social genocide
Weep now with the French, celebrate the coming restoration
Weep for the Uighur, who may not rise from the ashes

WINTER-SONG

The sharp claws of winter
Fall upon the carrion
Of my dwelling
Tearing apart its confidences

Spectral cold creeps across
Wetlands and blighted fields
Turning the crop's hair white
With its fatal bite

Autumn leaves flee
Leaving no fig-leaf cover
To protect the private parts
Of naked, defenceless trees

I hear winter's song
Moaning around the eaves
Telling of seasonal armies marching
To strip the earth of colour

In my warm cave I hear it
Listen to the wind, Nicodemus
It comes and goes where it will
Singing on its merciless way

Warm before Pentecostal coals
Fire upon my head
Reminded by this remembering song
Of resurrection pledge

BICYCLE

No one forgets how to ride a bicycle
Gripping the handlebars comes easily
Slipping onto the seat
Feet unerringly finding the pedals
The first gut wrenching effort
To get inert wheels moving

Riding over the rutted surface
Of a dirt road outside my son's house
On my grandson's bike
I raise dust of childhood memories
Wheels cracking ice over winter pools
On the frosty ride to school in Bendigo

Sweaty and hot, pushing up McIvor Road hill
Out to get dry scrub for Bonfire night
Potatoes raked out of the dying coals
Jet black
To be split open, butter and salt added
To burn too eager lips and tongue

The front wheel hanging still on
The designated hook in the undercroft
Of the boy's bicycle shed at High School
Foreshadowing the stillness
Of a final resting place long forgotten
In the mists of time

Now with the wind in my face
Sparkles flying from glinting spokes
Pursued by remembered shouts
Of teenage enthusiasm
At eighty-one, caution thrown to the wind
I hurtle downhill once again with uncertain brakes

ECHO

A rapid flight of bats, high intense cries sent forth
Bouncing back as screening, fragile whispers
Interpreted on rebound by sensitive receptors
A summoning voice to call forth a new world
Navigating through the crowded threat of space
Listening, filled, directed, guided by an echo

A stillness that has no returning sound
Deep into the well of silence, omitting all but what is found
Within the mysterious Kingdom of the mind
Shamans, monks, and contemplatives thrive alike
Flower-like, opening up as if to rain
Listening, filled, directed, just the same

A technical device, programmed to rule and to control
Not formed to hear an echo or to listen
No trust in hard earned knowledge or of caring wisdom
Non-conscious algorithm, dispensing with the human
Cold intelligence shearing off from consciousness
Claiming to know us better than we know ourselves

The beauty of bat flight, darkness glancing off the dipping wings
Blind to the light, listening into an echo
As holy ones intent upon the rhythm of unheard sound
Nurture the pulsing of an open, breathing heart
A listening that creates a centred world of love
Not artificial, cold, unmoved, efficient as the grave

REQUIEM

The Spanish mackerel leapt spangled
Into light
Luminous, iridescent in bright sun
Arched in glorious, transcendent flight
Scales gleaming, flashing, glinting
Splendid foam splash return
Glowing beauty gone from the sky

The Spanish mackerel leapt spangled
Into light
Luminous, iridescent in bright sun
Doomed
Arched in glorious, transcendent flight
Scales gleaming, flashing, glinting
Fate manacled
Lure fixed, line streaking to its goal
Tightens, foam splash return
Terminus
Beauty gone from the sky
Forever

DESERT

Ancestral home of all imagining
Memory of past things still cluster here
Stripped bare by excoriating sand-storm sand
Failures, cruelties, deceit and sorrow disappear
Cleansing to the bone of consciousness

The gift of aching silence in the barren waste
Gives focus to this meditation
Attending to what matters in the end
Cutting open protected isolation

Unveiling multiple pierces of loved others
That bind themselves together in our heart
That we might grow beyond a pale Narcissus
A listening waiting, gestating a fresh start

The desert is a call when life seems absent
A present distance that does not choose to wait
Nothing moves of daily tasks, intentions
The anchor point within the churning spate

Redefining destiny's decisions
Overpowering all the things of time-worn sense
Capitulation to a growing vision
Emergence of an undiluted yes

Bright star that sends its light to this abandoned place
Traveller across aeons from the birth of time
Carrying intimations of an unexpected Grace
Birthing a deathless hope of things divine

PROFIT FOR ALL

I am for peace
but when I speak
they are for war
Psalm 120:7

There is a loop, imprisoning as iron
Virtuous as virginity, shiny as righteousness
Jobs are sacrosanct, we generate them
By selling arms, a lucrative, rewarding choice

That protects our nation, elevates security
Dignifies sacrifice, preserves honour
Holds up freedom, provides jobs
Well targeted at the bottom line

Where was the decision made
To bond our nation with death merchants
To place Made in Australia stamped weapons
Into the hands of killers without qualms

Bringing death with dumb, blind conscience
To the defenceless young and innocent
Triumphantly crying, jobs, jobs, jobs
Without moral pause

Feeding on torn flesh, drinking fresh blood
Australian soup tasting of corpses

60,000 YEARS OLD

The young Aboriginal waitress
Greeted us warmly
Led us along the dappled verandah
To our table
Adjusted the settings
Took our order
Brought our food
Talked about the weather
Our journey
Said goodbye with a wide smile
And farewell wave
A 60,000 years old blessing

PULSE

We are stretched apart
A tug of war about to start

Singularity unique, communal whorls
The one and yet the all

Stamped until rocks crumble
Free moving, new in every tumble

Held by a force forever strong
Torn by the right, tied by the wrong

Horizontal, vertical, round and round
Trite to the height, in the depth profound

What is it that we are not seeing
Whence comes this pulse of being

FIRE

Fire licks across the trees
Wind urges it to greater feats
Unsatisfied hunger, consuming bees
Homes disappear in the merciless heat

All memories gone
Photographs of joy and peace
Blackened, destroyed, life prone
A future now beyond their reach

NIGHT IMAGININGS

Tendril brush awakens dozing senses
Feather touch calls forth instinctual ground
Barely a puff of timbral movement
Butterfly wings beat a flightless sound

No more substance than night's gentle kiss
Soft whisper in a silent room
Emanation of a vapour mist
Evasive as the silent hush of noon

Crystal tinkle of cold water trickling
Imagined horn in the dew wet dawn
Muffled cry in the evening glooming
Trembling echo of a new born fawn

A rustle in the curtain's falling
Inkling of an arrested breeze
Distant thunders quietly receding
Mouse scuttle in the hidden lees

Imagination's world constructed by the slightest noise
Tip-toeing by the bedroom door
A single string's vibrating poise
Forerunner of tomorrows promised score

BETWEEN

Here is the moment of ascendency
Here is the moment of our fall
Here is the sense of being present
Here is the sense of being absent from it all

Conscious of the moving sea, the salted air
Unaware of flow beneath the waves
Seeing light glint near and far
Not seeing what is lost and what is saved

Hearing across the void bird cries
Not hearing meanings distant echo
Awareness of the stars up in the sky
Unaware of destiny's tomorrow

We live in light and shadow
Within the strain of gain and loss
Coming full to harvest, lying fallow
Gold to be found beneath the dross

PARADOX

Is the fish in the water
Or the water in the fish
Is God in us
Or are we in God
Indivisible

Neither height nor depth
Far or near
Are separated in that oneness
Where one is all
And all is one

Every step out
Is a step in
Something Galaxy large
Something intrinsically small
Are at once together

At the beginning everything in that
Which has not yet come to be
Absence speaks of presence
Silence tells of the word
Distance and closeness side by side

In my image too
Image of all other people
United is to spell diversity
Uniqueness the form
Of every other thing

So I am here and there
Always a loved child who belongs
As all things do in the mind
Of the Eternal forever
Without separation

AUTUMN LEAVES

These autumn poems I write
Lift off the page, captured
By the mischievous seasonal wind
That sweeps up all things, whose destiny
Is to be set free into possibility
For their appointed task

I do not own these autumn leaves
Fondly, I hope they will prosper
Bringing rare beauty into the sharp air
Before the conquest of winter cold
The breeze giving them carriage
To lonely, waiting hearts, offering a hidden promise

Beautiful in the weakening sunlight
Falling gently to fertilise the earth
The very ground they call their own
Telling at once the story of this world
And its great secret of dying and rising again
The message of this autumnal wonder that surrounds us

OTHERWISE

To live otherwise is what we do
Turning our backs on slavery, on war
Taking up cudgels for the poor
The homeless, battered women
Abused children beyond the law

Trying to speak otherwise
To a deaf world, ears stuffed full
Sharing fragility and hospitality
Indifferent mobs devouring swill

Otherwise is being different
The slippery pole has no purchase
Nor truthfully the loud applause
Offered for conformity's compliance

We are otherwise
Looking for a new creation
Watching breeze ripple on water
God's promise to bring colour's trace
To the grey market place

FRAILTY

It is our fight against frailty
That is our undoing
As if we are anything else
But frail

Unfrail is a concept
That births and feeds hubris
Inviting us to overcome mortality
Believing it can be vanquished

Frailty encroaching
Is an invitation to rest
To float upon the water
Giving up strenuous laps

Learning that true power
Is not strength but wisdom
Welcoming, trusting
Drawing meaning we call spirit

DROUGHT

The morning mist is dry
Joining, parting, revealing, concealing
Dry as cremated ashes
Wind gusts carry no trace of moisture
A wind of autumn augurs winter spite
Bringing stale eucalyptus smells, dead leaves and dust

Water holes broken backed, crevasse crossed
Barren, endless barren paddocks, sere
Sheep carcasses rotting by the fence
Our neighbour hanged himself last year
In outback New South Wales a farmer in the mid-day heat
Shot his remaining herd and then himself

This is a sunburnt country, cracked, breaking
Glare runs bare-footed over punished soil
Tired, defeated workers, wives and children
Spread dry hay in listless toil
Defeated by implacable forces, stronger
Than their love for this beaten, suffering land

RECYCLED

It feels odd to be recycled
My atoms billions of years old
Stretching back millennia

What adventures they have had
Enterprises begun, projects explored
Voyages completed

Gathered now into this organic centre
Of blood and bone
Assembled to be me

Constant in their duty
Always at work
Sending incessantly electronic reassurance

How much I owe them
I do not know where I would be
If they had not paused for this short time

I hear them making plans
Some have already packed their bags
And moved on

But I will always be grateful
Under their guidance
I was able to hold myself together

A QUESTION TO KARL MARX

'Religion is the sigh of the oppressed creature, the heart of a heartless world, the soul of soulless conditions.'

Here is the irony
You sought to overcome injustice
Offering ideas that compounded it

You felt the pain of the people
Yet took away their heart and soul
Declaring their hope an opiate

You wrote in fire about equality
Planting inequality in countless fields
A harvest watered with blood

What lifts the sigh of the oppressed
What frees them from cruel history's grasp
Soulless conditions that crush their soul

If you could see now your heritage
Would you repudiate its tragic story
Because your heart's fire was love

PSALM

They attacked me in my youth
And in the long years of my age
Ploughing my life to its bone
Ploughing wide and deep furrows

I was bound with constricting cords
That tightened as the rain fell
Seeds will not grow, flowers blossom
If love is conditional

Who can endure such hate
Where the source of such malice
That delights in the suffering
Of those defenceless and without strength

Out of the bitterness life grew
We ate the fruit of our labour
Children grew around the table
As a vine the family flourished

There was forgiveness, healing and peace
A loaf broken, a cup filled
Those who passed by said of us
The blessing of the Lord is upon them

TUMBLING

It is tempting to believe
That the tide of time
Will wash the past away

It is equally tempting to believe
That the statue in the park
Will have importance for a new generation

Both are illusions cloaking
The reality we are
No extension beyond the now

Like the atoms that form us
What we have done
Tumbles into recreated newness

No longer alive or visible
But compelling in the imprint
Left upon the shape of things

For good or evil being there
Taken up, carried on, a casting
Present without definable recognition

Light that leads the way
That does not dazzle
Itself the path it illumines

That which is life moves on
Transformed, leaving behind
Darkness and no trace

Where in this will we be found
If not in God's wholeness
A place to dwell in the unknown

SILK CARPET

Small ruby centre
Four flaring petals circling
Bending leaves stretching out
Shedding in multifarious riot beyond

Temple design surrounding, reaching further
Enfolded in white, red, blue landscapes
Branches, flower freighted, spreading further into a rich wide land
Suddenly defined by tight ribboned borders

Deep channels of water connecting vines flowing
Within the layered boundary of intricate endings
Against the liminal edge, a deep red terminus, rectangle
Fringes at north-south ends, reaching further out

I walk, sinking into an oriental mind
Mystical, complex, holding all things in balance
By some elusive beauty of spirit flowing
Endlessly beneath my feet

WORRY BEADS

The time machine
Erroneously called worry beads
Is not difficult to use

Agile fingers stretch out space
Between the amber string
To break the force of *chronos*

That sense of time endlessly repeated
Iron locked to repetition
That keeps us imprisoned

Making space for *kairos*
That other sense of time
Dividing quantity from quality

That sense of time
Nurturing deep recollection
Loosing in our mind eternity

Kairos is God's time
Breaking into *chronos*
Redeeming loss

As I pass the coffee shop
Hearing beads clack
Spinning a web of purpose

I worry after all
That in time's repetition
I made little space for *kairos*

QUEST

Love seeks to stay alive out of the very soil
That seeks to negate it
Some great yearning that governs our toil
Profoundly more than customary habit

We shed snake skins of understanding
As we travel after
Reaching for meaning as the hungry for food
The thirsty for water

We set our sails guided by an unseen wind
That comes and goes
Is it that God is a hidden quest
Deep in our bones

Some are happy in safe harbours, others rejecting
That any quest exists
Out of the depths of daily struggle
There comes a siren song we can't resist

We push out again at the heart's dictate
No map entirely trustworthy
Setting our sails to the wind blowing
Into the rich golden sunset of possibility

Across water much travelled but not recorded
Guided by a natal star, green light alert
Travelling on the wide waterways of God
Within the human heart

VANTAGE POINT

If you follow the path
Past the memorial pond
Dedicated to the dead
Of forgotten wars

You will come to
A vantage point rock hewed
A viewing platform jutting out
Above the void

Eyes struggle to encompass the view
Its width and depth of horizon
Lost in the pale mist, sun soaked
Drenched above green with pastel colours

Down to the right, hill enfolded
Ruins of an ancient homestead
Grey with age, fire blackened
A tired, grieving chimney leaning forward

From this elevation looking out
Or by a turn looking down
Now and then collide
I am not sure which perspective is decisive

FLENSING KNIFE

Flensing floor blood ran in streams
Razor sharp knives cut blubber
From the dead stranded giants
Killed instantly by a harpoon's explosive charge

So pervasive the smell of this slaughter
It penetrated the skin of workers
Who carried the foul odour of their trade
With every step, a deep irremovable signature

What we do over time
Seeps into our skin, the heart of us
Carrying the trace of all that
We have done for good or ill

A deep inescapable imprint
Pervading the whole, tattooed, ingrained
Time etches the sum of all our deeds
Into the fibre of our being

Washing of hands, heartfelt confession
Cannot remove what choice has sculptured
Into the foundation of our life
Here the flensing knife has no power

POLLUTION

Are stranded whales
Canaries of the sea
Pods beach-cast in despair
Their life-habitat now deadly

Encountering a rainbow parrot
Dead upon the path
I looked for its assassin
Only polluted air

The slow dying of our Village emblem
The growling grass frog
Is sign of the fading health
Of our beloved wet-lands

As if sea, land and air
Are succumbing to our greed
New Delhi prepares for winter
School children in class breathe through face masks

QUEENS COLLEGE

The College squats solidly
As it always has
Time's stain undetectable
On its outward features

Sixty years gone since I first
Entered its venerable gates
With eager anticipation
And tremulous fears

Now a museum of recollection
Long corridors, remembered stairs
Sunlight dappling the Chapel
With soft colours through stained glass

A wind of memory blows embers
Into life, warm, flickering, glowing
A spoon bashing cohort of adolescents
Loud, bewildered, indolent

Not yet aware of subtle influences
Shaping, directing, forming, pointing
Laying out roads, paths, byways
Along which their life will travel

A vast garden, natives and exotics
Gathered around the tree of knowledge
Treacherous weeds of intellectual arrogance
And social elitism ready to bloom

As I cross the quadrangle
I hear shouts and greetings
Of present inhabitants in small rooms
Today's coterie of ambition and hope

For an instant I am one of them
Looking out at an uncrossed country
To be entered, cultivated, celebrated
A future yet to be, already cast

Standing in this familiar place
A distant mirror of loved images
There is a moment of believing I will understand
All that is gathered in this stillness

AFTER THOMAS MERTON

Inspired by passages from THE WATERS OF SILOE.

Who can dwell at ease in a culture
Dedicated to the pursuit of shadows
Where, muffin like, trumpeted values crumble
In your hands
Pleasures of the media world shrink, disappear
Die young
Platitudinous clichés of reconciliation
Turn constantly to war

Who will tell us that truth's fish
Cannot be caught in the shallows
Or that love only increases when given away
Pouring itself out for others, spring rain of life itself
That the secret love of money is as delusional
As the expectation your fame will last beyond a generation

There is a gladness that has more joy
Than the laughter of thousands
A silence more eloquent than all the fine
Spun words of politicians and aspiring leaders
Contentment and rest not dependent on
Foam rubber mattresses and leather lounges

There is deep in the heart a spoken-for
The going out to return from whence it came
A centre spiralling into eternity
Where beauty and actuality of all things
Lies nested in the real
Balm of all that is
From which all things come and to which
All things return

VOICE

Born into the white noise of existence
We begin at once to draw forth
Harmony and rhythm scoring the
Understandings of a burgeoning self
Orchestrating the symphony of our lives
With many sounds, many instruments
Calling into focus the music of our being
Putting together a multi-layered self

Held by a central theme
      stated,
            reshaped,
                  replayed,
                        rehearsed
Conch shell of spoken mystery
      that is the self's expression
            This deciding centre
                  subsidiary awareness recognises
                      no matter what is said
Cadence,
      timbre,
            faint trembling music of beyond
Trace of the muse that gathers us in
      made evident in educated sounds
Someone becoming
      out of the reservoir of potentiality

To form,

    to shape,

        to bring to life

            out of blank sound that voice

                which is our self

our given task

Hearts leap at the hearing of your voice
Articulated depth of spirit
Who-ness in communication
Personal questing, unfolding otherness
Finding your own voice has been the work of years
That voice speaks of the whole of you
That comes to me now
The gift of your authentic self

ROCK ART

Art, sign of civilisation
Second creation on rock and stone
Birth of the mind's expansion
Representing blood and bone

Securing place, securing time
Reaching for a world becoming
Spreading out encoded patterns
Making real perceptual seeming

Ochre mouth-sprayed on a wall
Icons painted by frayed sticks
Hidden in the mist of aeons
Life rising up beyond life's risk

Shaman bodied, sacred calling
To capture spirit in cave lime
Spirit womb of human beings
Life painting life sublime

Abundant flow, creative image
Shaped into a human face
Presence speaking out of darkness
Light transforming inert space

Transcendence in the slender line
A scratch upon eternity
Explosion of awakening thought
Trembling touch of certainty

Ritual dancing, social tracing
Promise of a coming time
Pointing to the heart of mystery
Proclaiming vision of the blind

Here the poetry of our kind
Beauty in its primal form
Holding treasure of the soul
Evaporating in a mobile storm

DIGGER

He asked them not to let him die alone
A promise he had kept a thousand times
Hold my hand for touch will be my solace
Memory held past moments in his eye

Death called regularly on the Burma railway
They died gaunt, starved, beaten, fighting disease
A contract rose among them. All assented
No one would be left to die his death alone

He was a rare survivor of that bitter scene
Now come to his last moments in his turn
He saw again the gathered crowd of mourners
They held their comrade's hand until the end

The hospital bed surrounded by his family
His plea from the deepest fibre of his being
With love and tears they held his hands, together
The promise lived, he did not die alone

SUNDIAL

The flower sundial
Casts its shadow line
Across numbered petals
In its circled haven

Predictability masking complexity
Elliptical projection over time
Short dark reach now, endless stretching then
Responsive to unseen cosmic forces

Unsettling this phantom permanence
Minuet of dark and light
We are placed, in step, within its magic
Timeliness balancing endless variables

Could it be that time
Is no other than light and dark
In patterned sequence
Into which we are called
By the deep music of the dance

TRAFFIC JAM

Inch by inch we move
Temperatures in metal cages rise
Specimen butterflies pinned to a traffic board
Helpless we seek to blame, to curse, despise

Surrounding drivers constitute a threat
Edging into tight space to advantage
Occupying air more properly mine
Anxiety concerning dismantled plans on rampage

Edging just a little further
Constrained by roaring verbal fervour
Physics squeezes wired bodies
What are the means to mediate distress

Time crawls past, empty, futile, kept
Powerless to gain a further place
An agitating stillness to restrain
Distractions have no comfort food within

Broiling in the stomach cauldron
Building flame within the mind
A consuming banking fire
Smoking frustration and thwarted desire

Inevitability smugly reigns supreme
Harsh introduction to lurking victimhood
Handcuffed hands, ankle-chained feet
Car engines blow out wasted fuel unspent

Rain starts to fall, blind vision now within the tent
Windows stain, a ribboned blind
Silent watches turn to ticking loudly
Spirits harden, dry cast off orange rind

There is an end to unexpected bondage
Rain will cease, the sun will shine, wheels turn again
A choked road cleared of debris will be found
All around the same pitying cry, Dear God, Why me

A flattened surface swept of options
A caterpillar line of fundament
Humanity cannot escape predicament
Turning a key leaves wanting still unmet

MIRROR-IMAGE

The small boy
Looks into the mirror
Freezes
So does the image

He looks behind the mirror
Runs away
Sneaks back to peer
Around the edge

Sees himself
Looking back
He runs behind again
Stands mystified
Returns
As does the image
He jumps
He falls

Spreads arms
Wide
As does the image
Persisting mirage

He does not know
Yet
That all his life
He will ask

Is that me
Who am I
What is real
What is illusion

THE ROAD LEADS...

I set off along the road
Beside the stream, over the hill
Nothing to ease the load
Each day will be well

There is here tasked need
I do not know
Where it will lead
Except through wind and snow

Rap upon the hostel door
Warm light of welcoming
Darkness descends much as before
Pause for recovering

The road leads over the hill
Is it destiny's choice
Hear the calling bell
Listen to its voice

Time to be afoot
Time again for travelling
Time for shade and rest
Life's riddle unravelling

I am content in seeking
One foot, one step to follow
There is a waiting
The rising of tomorrow

AFTER

A STITCH IN TIME

On this bleak day, perversely good
A stitch in time on Roman wood

Contorted by the wracking pain
Needle in the wounded side
Gasping for life giving breath
Stitching close, stitching wide

Here a stitch in time
A fraying universe
Holding together diverse worlds
Sealing of creation's birth

Love's thread folding tightly
A bleeding leaking life
Bringing to its healing
Diseased estrangement, inner strife

In time's nick a binding
Saving task is being done
Stitch that is still piercing
Uniting distance into one

Antiseptic for our wounds
Closing off disease and death
A stitch in time regardless
Of consequence or cost

On this bleak day, perversely good
A stitch in time on Roman wood

TRANSLATION

If silence is the language of God
Silence does not speak with clarity
Leaving us a discerning task
What is it we must do

We risk a judgment
Of God's intention
Not easily codified into
Assured projection

Evolving into understanding
By indwelling silence
Coming to realise
Participation leads to translation

CURRENT

The boat of our life
Travels on an eternal river
What floats it
Is beyond our ken

Consciousness ubiquitous
Defying explanation
Deep in the stream
Love carries its hidden meaning

How explain community
Or tell each other what it is
We cannot control memory
Or escape its spell

Below the boat
Nothing to be seen
Netted or caught
A current in which all life flows

FEAST

The sense of fragmentation
Is a forgetting
The pulling apart is a fault
Of not remembering

So many paths lead back
To the one destination
So many songs celebrate
That which we deeply know
But cannot tell

If we ask why are we
So scattered and cast about
I would reply
We have lost our way
To that hidden wholeness
That waits for our return

Our failure is not listening
To the echo of our heart's silence
We miss the gesture that points
To footprints which if followed
Will lead us home

To that open table and a feast
Where we and God break bread
Together
With undiminished joy

WEAVER OF DREAMS

A weaver of dreams was Jesus
Tossing off stories, making a world
In which our humanness might thrive

Creating a universe of meaning
That persuasively offers balance
In the fragmentation of social incoherence

We still live in that storied realm
Finding gossamer tendrils drifting
That bind us to a burgeoning purpose

Not defeated by brutal injustice
Or cruel indifference to the wretched
Holding with the dream love brings

CAVE

Out of death's underworld
Cave darkness surrounding
Diving within deadly currents
Of the river Styx

Rock panic, primordial, deep rooted fear
Holding to the umbilical cord desperately
Led along the treacherous birth canal
Of brittle, life sucking stone

Bursting into air and light
Out of death's dark kingdom
'I am the resurrection and the life'
Says the Lord. 'Celebrate with me'

MOON

A luscious pumpkin of a moon
Larger than imagination
Opening up a shining way
In that dark night as we
Walked home from the movies

A country road, tho' children
We did not fear demons
In the bushes, threats or dangers
What is it doing there I wondered

Not realising that I was not
Asking questions of it
This glorious pock-faced other
Was asking questions of me

MINISTRY

Ten years of careful study
A comprehensive intellectual course
Countless hours of discussion, sturdy
Conviction fighting what seems perverse

The weekly preaching of the Word
Using a rusted, ancient sword
Daily caring for a people
Underneath a gothic steeple

Forty years a Minister ordained
Still struggling to reduce the pain
Of lukewarm calm, measured indifference
A desire to cry out what of the pestilence

One image keeps ministry retained
A hand once on the plow, fidelity sustained
Looking back on what defines the quest
A sowing time, a coming harvest yet

REALM

The realm of God is
You cannot drive to its limits
It has no limits

You cannot evade its claim
For you are a citizen
With responsibilities and tasks

Should you go to extremes
To escape your taxes
They will await your return

The Kingdom is all inclusive
Both outside and inside
It has no loopholes

Presence cannot be diminished
Defined or de-valued
It is what it is

We have a free choice
To name ourselves as belonging
To sing the universal anthem wholeheartedly

AUTHORITY

Few people have authority
He certainly did, in spades
The cast of his words
Physical presence
Aura of assurance

There was stillness
When he spoke
Bewitching, as if listeners
Were enfolded in a net
Of attentive compulsion

A choice that required
Nothing less than everything
That brooked no refusal
If humanness was to bloom

No one knows more
Of the truth than
They are of the truth
Sören wrote plaintively

We moved from words
To those things done
Destination reached at last
In who he was

So totally compelling
In a moment of madness you
Felt that by touching him
You would be made whole

As if the secrets of the depths
Would rise up naked to
Our gaze, illuminated
To whisper you are free

Bird flight, leaf green
Mushroom circle, tender stream
Echo rich, word perfect
In the moment of saying yes

NONCHALANCE

Giggling greeting, lovely fey creatures
In fluffy coloured dresses
Regarding all seriousness with
A rare nonchalance
Obsessed by glints on fresh nail polish
Selfies consumed with passionate intensity
Consternation at scarlet ribbons awry
On the new green dress
Happily blossoming within a minutiae bubble

So would it be watching lichen
Inch up the concrete wall of
The wetland's surround
Ducks lazily engaged with the
Sprinkling fountain for no good reason
I wonder at their easy fascination
Captivated I listen for distant news
Summoned by inescapable depth
The egret stone still, as if spaced out

APRIL FOOL

They are much entertained by the irony
April Fool's day falls on Resurrection Sunday
Celebrating that the calendar this year
Declares what has always been true
The foolishness of believing absurdity

Not understanding that only a fool
Has the wisdom to render absurd
Pretensions of the clever and complacent
Raising the question about the meaning of
Cap and bells on this day of love's transparency

BEING

What is meant by being, he asked
The question attesting to its is-ness

Actuality confronts us, I thought
With two faces, presence and potentiality

The one indubitably there
The other a not yet-ness coming

Is this a shadow play of God, he said
This being and this becoming

Out of the fire an answer
Naming what we call God

I am what I am
I will be what I will be

Life, the unity of becoming and being
Actuality, the handprint of the One

BEGINNING

Do not leave us without you
Fibre of our being-ness
We are reaching after
Returning to the nest
A flight from darkness
Into light and darkness
Yet again
We must now begin
To love in truthfulness

CHRISTMAS

Christmas gathering
Telling of the birth
Holding on to joy
Child of priceless worth

A world of mystery
Occasion to rejoice
Incense cloud of gladness
A matter of our choice

Focus on a manager
Ox and cow and ass
Lantern in the darkness
Leading to the pass

Out across the valley
Eyes looking for the road
Seeing only roman trees
Holding human loads

Hear the ringing bells
Listen to the trumpet sound
Joy in heaven and hell
Our lost world is found

REGRET

After a lifetime of ministry
I regret that I wrote
And spoke so much about
The faith that is believed
And so little of
The faith by which we believe
That light touch of love
On the sleeping head of a child
The gentle suffering thing
At the heart of all experience

LIGHT

All is in motion
Ghost particles to gigantic worlds
Travelling endlessly
The possible made real
By the impossible
Creative power
That animates our deepest sense
Of being

Making conscious that what we know
Is unbelievable
We can only embrace
Or not embrace God
Other options are
But swirls
Illusionary movements
Of all things in motion

EASTER BLOCK

The laser pares away the unnecessary, cutting into the
        wood block,
crafting a planned image of the wooden self, programmed
        without emotion
to a destined end, where out of the tree's beneficence is carved
        a victim
effigy, to be polished, painted, given a semblance of life by
        artifice, destined
to stand motionless before the mirror, peering blankly into a
        barren soul, much
sought after as our deepest desire, an Easter gift, quite cheap,
        representing another
manufactured form well fit for crucifixion, unlikely to rise as
        challenge to the
assembly line of unreal things without a heart, costing no more
        than thirty silver
pieces

MAGPIE SONG

Magpie song wakes the morning up
Broken, wandering, incomplete, uncertain
Reminding us that richness waits
By its very indecisiveness issuing a warning

We are not Captains of our fate
Masters of our soul, invincible before
Malignant and destructive forces
That we must rise above and banish

In their melodic chaos magpies
Know that out of possibilities
Of each day we stumble, sometimes fail
Never quite achieving completion that we seek

Still they sing, their very incapacity
Bringing a startling beauty
Not perfect, not satisfying, not complete
But in its shared trajectory triumphant

CARD PLAYING

What is intuitive
Is my own sense of being
In this now

Of God not the intuitive alone
Unveiling that which demonstrates
What is

As to what I know
Of things present
Blind senses testify

These modes of experience
Carry an address
Which cannot be avoided

Looked in the eye
I learn what I could not discover
I am seized irrevocably

So this self, this Other, this moment
Are one around a table playing cards
An empty chair waiting to be occupied

WHY IS IT SO?

She does not want to eat
Or get dressed
Sleeping in her dressing gown
Through the long morning

Complaining of the refrigerator shouting at her
Phantom plates breaking in the sink
Telling him to walk the dog
Dead, these long years past

Married fifty years
She a child again
Fretful, uncertain, impossible
He stands immobile
In the lounge room

Distress, bewilderment
Rage and sadness intermingle
He looks at their wedding photograph
Seeing strangers unrecognised

It is 6.30 p.m.
Time for pills in sequence
Marshalling for the nightly fight
Asking 'Why is it so?'

SPACE

There is endlessness in inner and outer space
The traveller will find no event horizon
In which direction and momentum collide

Organisms tenuous in cold absence
Numberless populations of the inorganic thrive
Without assurance of escape from loneliness

Space filled with soundless rhythm
Ancestor particles replicating trajectories
In energetic microcosms, here, not here, here

Black holes sucking potentiality into themselves
Ephemeral loci mysteriously alert
To sentient life

Is it possible to conceive participation
From these trackless voids. To meet, to talk
To dialogue, kindled by the warmth of fire

Where is the harvest?

FAKE

How discern between the fake and true
Or decide between the straightly old and the deceitful new
I grip your hand, you have my solemn word
Today such integrity seems palpably absurd

A time that disdained froth and dross
Commitment meant the pledging of a troth
But now the truly smart know how to counterfeit a fake
Morals are no barrier to being on the make

All for the purpose of creating an advantage
To magnify the sparkle of a diamond sharpened image
Twisting and turning is a salesman's gift
Between the ideal and the surreal is but a minor rift

Why bother whether cant erodes confided trust
There is no force in ought or must
We conjure up ingredients that seem
trustworthy, cleverness the source of our esteem

What we seek is to be both strong and wealthy
There is no ultimate beyond the latest selfie
Do not make of honesty and fakery an issue
I am committed to my life of see-through tissue

Cornucopia of plenty
Bottomless the empty

JESUS

They crucified Jesus because
He was an enigma
Forget the politics
They could not lay a glove on him
On his soul, on his vision

No means emerged to tame
His poetic sense of otherness
Once set free
They could not pin him down
Or domesticate his wildness

That disturbed the law mercilessly
They had to protect form by
Destroying substance
Substituting Imperial decree
For the lilies of the field

Convinced that disturbance of
The set order was threatening
Decorum and structural verities
Declining the invitation
To board the tram

What he was doing
Was planting seeds
That grew into trees of life
Fed by rivers from creation's dawn
Fertilised by the people's hope

MY NAME IS ...

Gathered around, the small baptismal group
Out of poverty offering their gift
One by one, children of an old belonging
My name is...
Sounding out baptism's gift
You are one with us

My name is ... should you need a friend
My name is ...the offer fetching and carrying
My name is ...if needed chopping wood
The litany goes on around the circle
Offering what they can, though small it is
My name is ...

Here is the source of what unites
The spoken name says we belong
Loved and loved in return
I will be for you, sister, brother
One within this family out of time
We belong together, our name is ...

SONG-SPELL

I imagine Jesus as a young man
Singing
As he walked the dusty roads
Of Palestine sun splashed
Delighting in the children's laughter
The bright lilies of the field
Pausing to watch the casting
Of seed, tomorrow's harvest

Unaware of small clouds gathering
Drawing strength, growing in size
Blocking the sun on that fateful day
When darkness covered the face
Of the earth
The true son of God
Singing his songs
Birthing a new creation